Kindergarten

CAN YOU FIND ME?

Building Thinking Skills
Reading • Math • Science • Social Studies

SERIES TITLES
Can You Find Me? PreK
Can You Find Me? K

Written by
Michael Baker, Cheryl Block

Illustrated by
Eric Cardinale

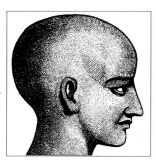

© 2003
CRITICAL THINKING BOOKS & SOFTWARE
www.CriticalThinking.com
P.O. Box 448 • Pacific Grove • CA 93950-0448
Phone 800-458-4849 • FAX 831-393-3277
ISBN 0-89455-794-7
Printed in China

INTRODUCTION

The riddles in this book develop thinking skills as students learn math, reading, science, and social studies. These activities are fun as well as educational. They engage students in learning, develop listening skills, and require critical thinking. They also provide you with many opportunities to teach children new concepts and information related to the different riddle topics.

The riddles should be read aloud. They are not designed to be used by students independently. Students can answer orally or point to the correct answer. You may need to reread a riddle and prompt a student with questions that focus him/her on important information (clues) necessary to solve the riddle. For optimal academic benefit, you should question and discuss not only your student's answer but also the thinking he or she used to solve the riddle.

You may find the Sample Lesson on page iv helpful. The Skills Matrices at the end of the book identify the educational standards and thinking skills used in each activity.

TABLE OF CONTENTS

SAMPLE LESSON

Read aloud the riddle on the next page. Explain that one of the pictures is the answer. Ask your student/child if he or she knows the answer to the riddle.

If the student answers correctly:

Point to the dog and ask the student why the dog cannot be the answer. If the student cannot explain why the dog is not the correct answer, then read each clue one by one so the student can deduce that the dog is not the correct choice because it has short legs. Next, point to the camel and repeat the process. The student should be able to explain that the camel is not the correct choice because it does not have spots. Finally, point to the giraffe and have the student explain that the giraffe is the correct choice because it has four long legs, a long neck, *and* spots. If the student cannot remember the reasons, repeat the clues one by one.

If the student answers incorrectly:

1. Read the first clue in the riddle: *I have four long legs.* Ask the student to look at each picture to see if the animal has long legs. Once the student concludes that the dog does not have long legs then make sure that the student understands that the dog cannot be the picture we are looking for. The answer is either the giraffe or the camel because they both have long legs.

2. Read the next clue: *And a long neck too.* Ask the student to look at the giraffe and camel to see if each animal has a long neck. Once the student concludes that both animals have long necks, be sure the student understands that the answer is still either the giraffe or camel.

3. Read the next clue: *My skin has spots.* Ask the student to look at the giraffe and camel to see which animal has spots. Once the student concludes that the giraffe has spots and the camel does not, then make sure the student understands that the riddle is solved. The giraffe is the animal that fits all the clues.

Additional suggestions for effective questioning:

1. When the student indicates that he/she doesn't understand the question, rephrase the question to clarify it. Do not ask the same question again.

2. When the student answers a question incorrectly, ask him or her to explain the answer. If there is a misunderstanding of the question, clarify the question. If there is a lack of understanding of the content, go back to the riddle and ask a question on the content.

3. Direct and guide the student to the answer rather than simply telling him or her.

SAMPLE LESSON

I have four long legs
And a long neck too,
My skin has many spots,
You see me at the zoo.

Of the three things that you see,
Tell me now, can you find me?

I'm showing four fingers
My two hands are raised high.
My shoes have six eyelets each
And laces that I must tie.

Of the three people that you see
Tell me now, can you find me?

I'm taller than Amy

So I'm not the smallest.

I'm taller than Dion

But I'm not the tallest.

Of the four people that you see

Tell me now, can you find me?

Two of us have the same shape
We're as tall as we are wide.
I'm the one turned on my corner
Instead of on my side.

Of the four things that you see
Tell me now, can you find me?

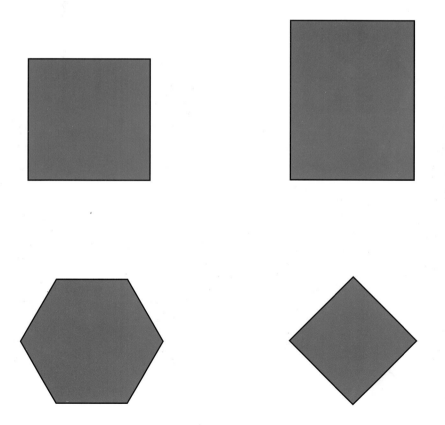

With one I make two

With two I make three.

Of the four numbers that you see

Tell me now, can you find me?

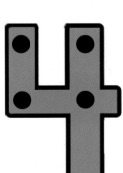

If I had two pigs   and was given this many more

I'd have more pigs than would fit through this door.

Of the three numbers that you see
How many pigs belong to me?

  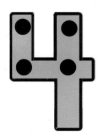

Sam is the first in line
Yuki is at the end.
My friend Jan is the third
Can you find my friend?

I have one hand on my side

And one hand on my shoe.

I'm sitting on a rectangle

With three sides that are blue.

Of the four pictures that you see

Tell me now, can you find me?

There are two in this family and no more
They have straight lines two, three, or four.
Of the different shapes that you see
Which two shapes must these two be?

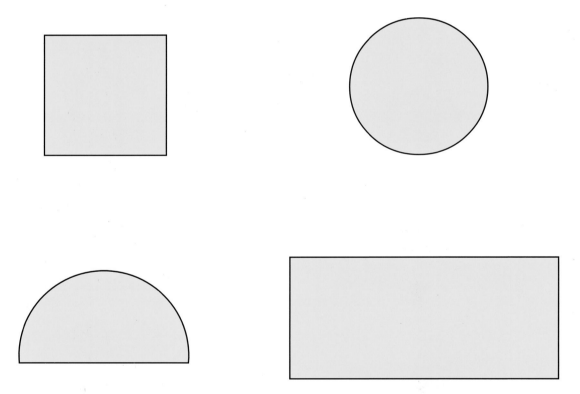

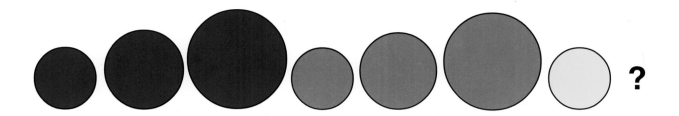

These circles have a pattern
Look at each one in the row.
Which circle comes next?
Can you find it below?

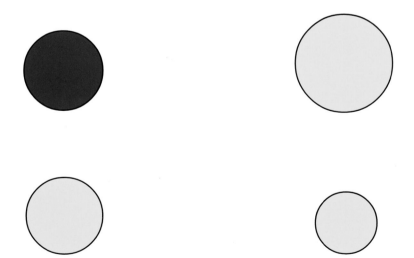

I have one more than three
Jo has two less than me.
Of the groups you see below
Which group belongs to Jo?

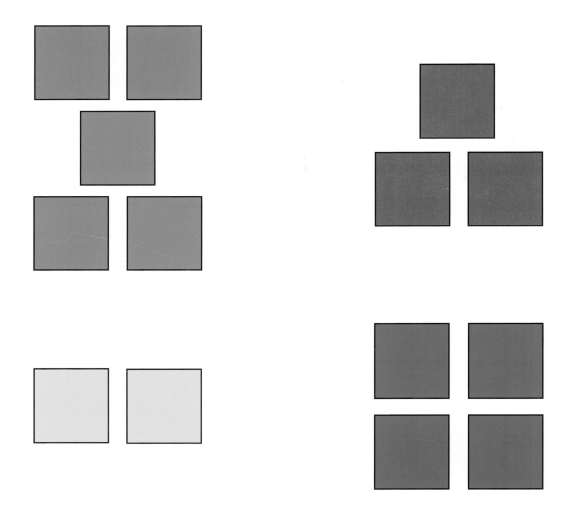

I am less than five

But I am more than three.

I'm a number below

Which number must I be?

  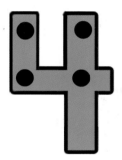

I am a number

That comes after three.

I am greater than six

Eight is greater than me.

Of the four numbers that you see

Tell me now, can you find me?

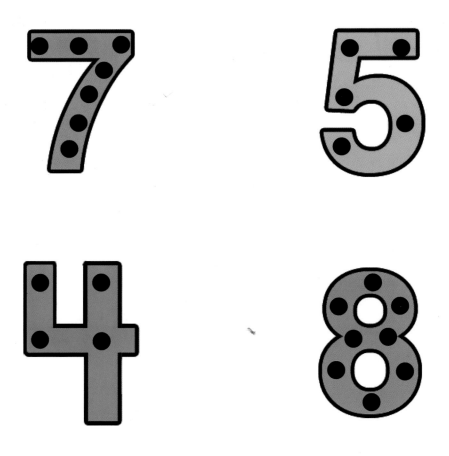

Counting Animals at the Pound

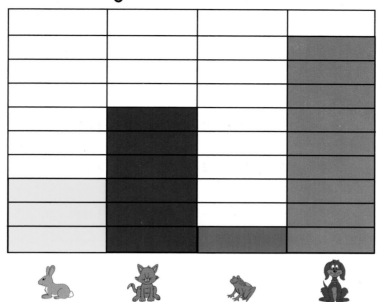

Number of animals counted

Joe spends the day at the city pound

Counting the animals that have been found.

Of all the animals that he sees

The chart shows he counted the most of these.

Of the four choices you see below

Which one does the answer show?

I'm hiding in the shapes

Can you figure out where?

I'm under a triangle

On the left of a square.

Of the four pictures that you see

Tell me now, can you find me?

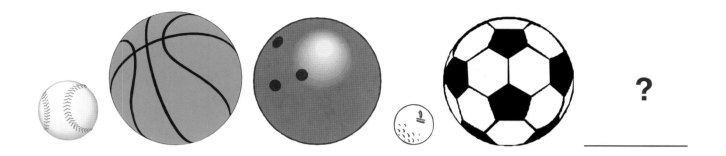

These balls have a pattern
Look at each in the row.
Which ball should come next?
Can you find it below?

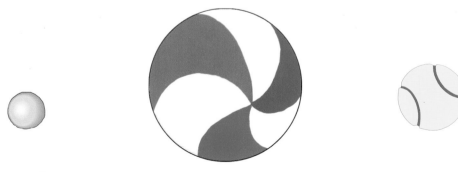

Our Favorite Fruit

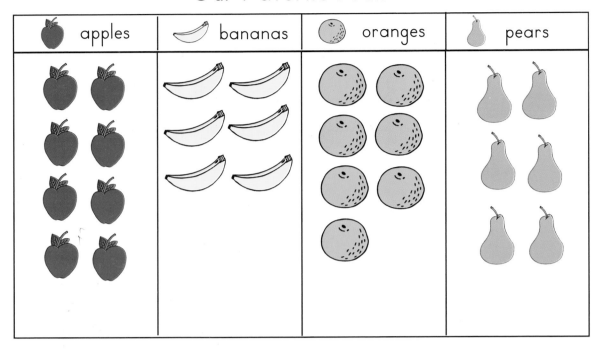

apples	bananas	oranges	pears

Each student picked a favorite fruit
And placed it with the rest.
Apples, oranges, bananas, or pears
Which fruit was liked the best?

Of the four fruits that you see
Which kind of fruit must this be?

I am in the middle row
One of three girls on the right.
I have yellow hair and socks
And my tee shirt's blue and white.

Of all the girls that you see
Tell me now can you find me?

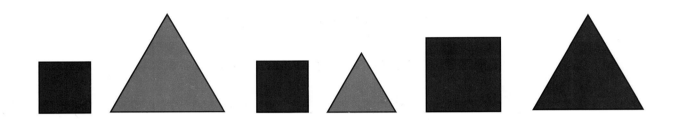

These objects have a pattern
Is it shape, size, or color?
Look carefully at these figures
What pattern can you discover?

shape   **size**   **color**

I have one more than three
Gus has one less than me.
Count my blocks and those of Gus
Which group of blocks belongs to us?

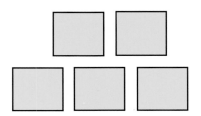

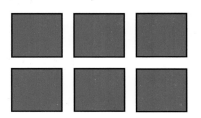

Chu   Lupe   Jeremy   Me

Chu has 3 pennies
Jeremy has a dime.
Lupe has two nickels
But one of them is mine.

Of Jeremy, Chu, Lupe, and me
Which of us has the most money?

Bill ate part of the apple
Then left half for his friend Jim.
Jim ate half of what was left
And saved the rest for Tim.

Look at the pictures of this healthy treat
Then point to the one that Tim got to eat.

Jim wears the shirts in the blue circle
Shirts in the green circle are worn by Joe.
How many shirts are worn by both boys?
The answer can be seen below.

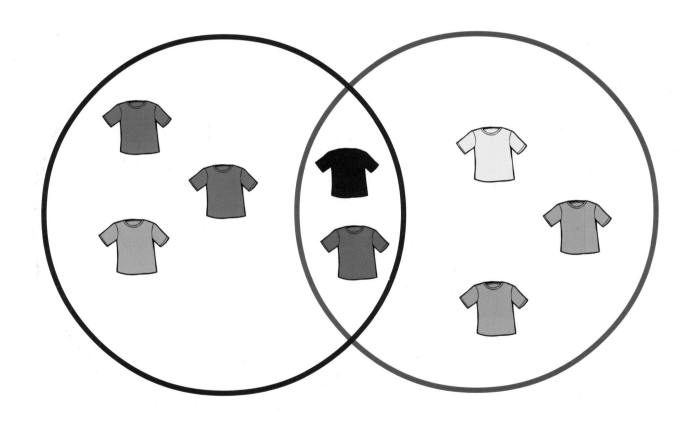

Jim can wear socks that have some red
Zach can wear socks that have some blue.
How many socks can both boys wear?
The socks in both circles are your clue.

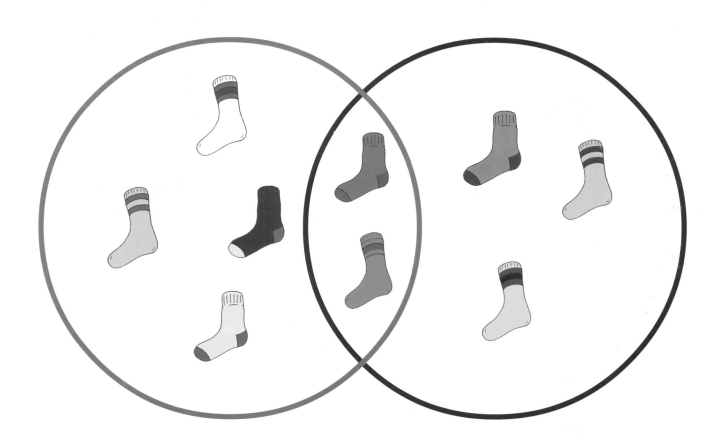

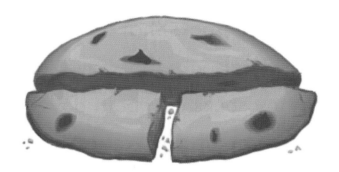

Bill left half a cookie
Jasmine ate half of that.
Denise found what was left
And handed it to Pat.

Who had the largest piece?
Bill, Jasmine, Pat, or Denise?

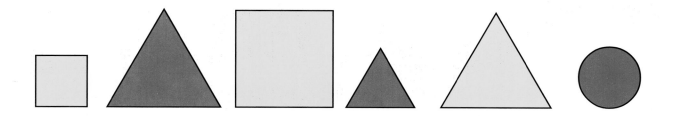

These figures have a pattern
Is it shape, size, or color?
Look carefully at these figures
What pattern can you discover?

shape   **size**   **color**

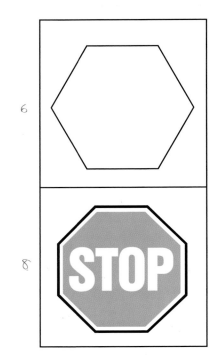

6

8

?

Look at each pair of pictures
There's always two of a kind.
Find how each pair is alike
Then you'll know what to find.

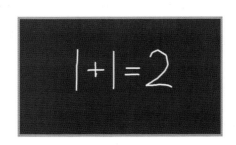

I get to drive a racing car
And I can hardly wait!
I'm not the first or second
I'll be third to pass the gate.

Of the four cars that you see
Tell me now, can you find me?

These three shapes are lost

Their families are below.

See how each family looks alike

To see where each shape should go.

Point to where each shape should go

Then tell my why you know it's so.

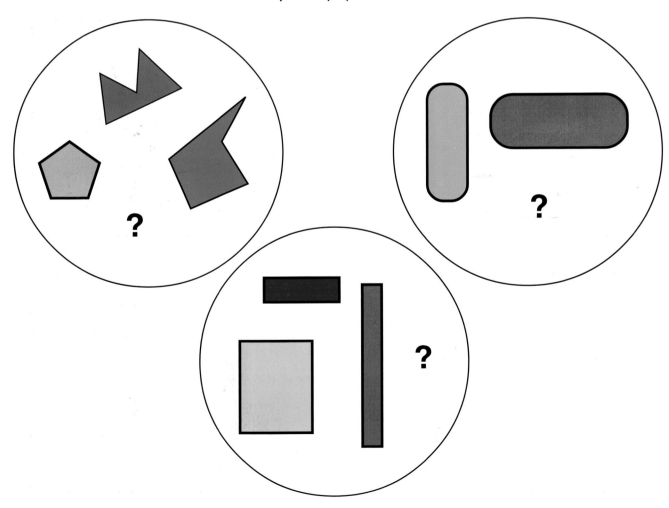

On the left is a big striped cat

Who always wears a purple hat.

On the right is a green and white frog

Who rides atop a shaggy dog.

Of the four groups that you see

Which group must this one be?

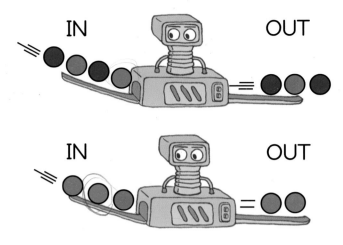

IN   OUT

This machine eats dots

It is a special tool.

See what goes in and out

Can you figure out its rule?

If you feed it this group below

Which group will come out, do you know?

IN   OUT

?

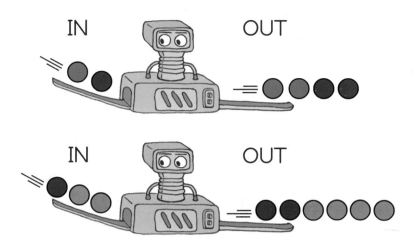

This machine adds dots

It is a special tool.

See what goes in and out

Can you figure out its rule?

If you feed it this group below

Which group will come out, do you know?

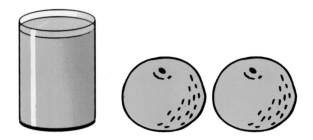

I squeezed two oranges
To fill the glass you see.
How many more must I squeeze
To fill these other three?

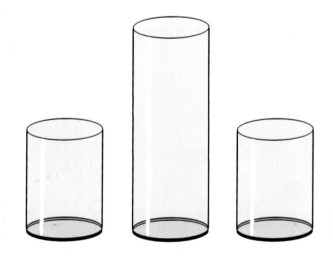

I ate half an apple

I ate a whole pear.

I wanted more cherries

But there were only five there.

Of the four kids that you see

Tell me now, can you find me?

If I am wearing black
I'm with Bill and Tom.
If I am wearing red
I'm with Bill and Mom.

Me

Careful now, Tom dresses just like me.
You must use logic to find the right three.

What are two things
A plant needs to grow?
Look at the pictures
Can you find them below?

These pictures tell a story
But not in the order you see.
Tell me what must have happened
As you point to them one, two, three.

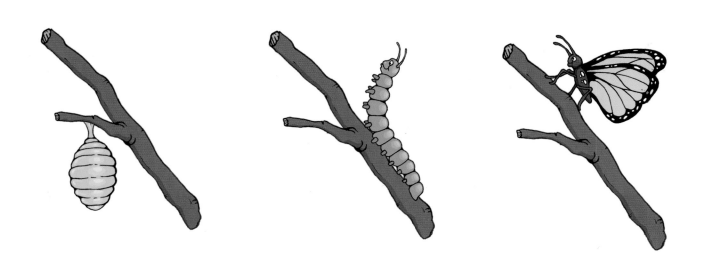

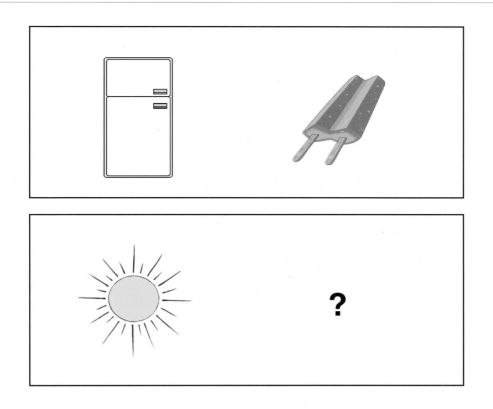

In each pair of pictures

You will see

From the first picture in the box

What the next one should be.

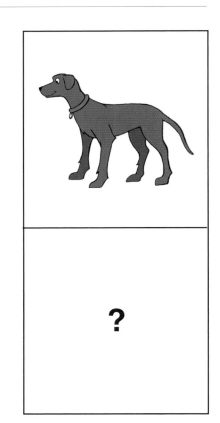

?

Look at each pair of pictures
There's always two of a kind.
Find how each pair is alike
Then you'll know what to find.

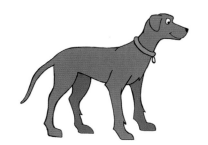

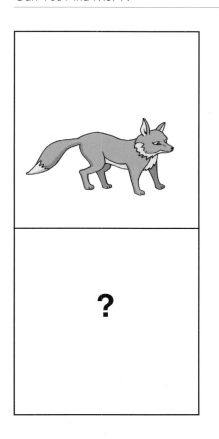

Look at each pair of pictures
There's always two of a kind.
Find how each pair is alike
Then you'll know what to find.

With the three pictures
That you see
Put them in order
One, two, three.

1.

2.

3.

A shark has so many
A toddler has a few.
You will lose your first set
As the second pushes through.

Of the three objects that you see
Tell me now, can you find me?

  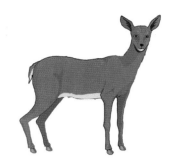

These three animals are lost

Their homes are shown below.

Point to where each one lives

Then tell me how you know.

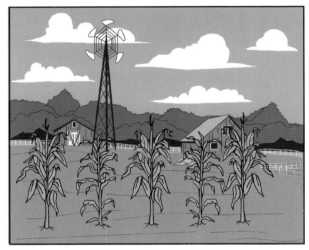 

Three of my gills are easy to see
My belly is colored white.
My open mouth shows seven teeth
And I am on the right.

Of the four sharks that you see
Tell me now, can you find me?

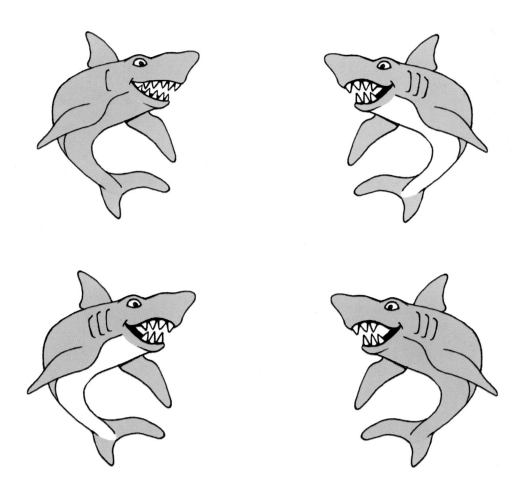

These pictures tell a story
But not in the order you see.
Tell me what must have happened
As you point to them one, two, three.

I can outrun a horse
And I stand eight feet high.
I have large wings
But I cannot fly.

Of the four pictures that you see
Tell me now, can you find me?

A toad ate a beetle.
A lizard ate the toad.
A hawk ate the lizard
When it tried to cross the road.

Of the four pictures that you see
Which shows the end of the sad story?

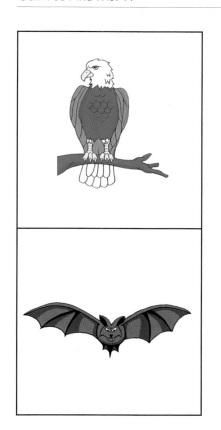

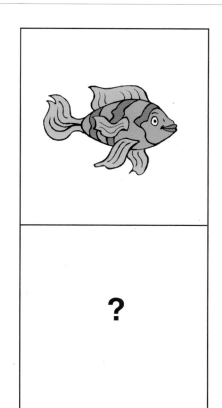

?

Look at each pair of pictures
There's one you must find.
The clue is in the pictures
There's always two of a kind.

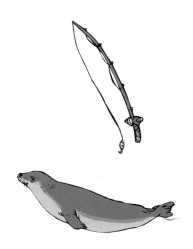

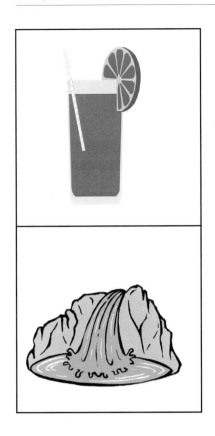

Look at each pair of pictures

There's one you must find.

The clue is in the pictures

There's always two of a kind.

These pictures show a pattern.
Look at each one in the row.
What should the next picture be?
It is one of those below.

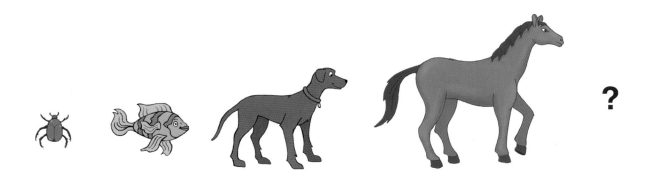

These pictures show a pattern
Look at each one in the row.
What should the next picture be?
It is one of those below.

These pictures show a pattern
Look at each one in the row.
What should the next picture be?
It is one of those below.

It rained all day
Then rained all night.
Then finally there
Was bright sunlight.

Which group of pictures that you see
Tells what happened in this story?

These three animals are lost
Their families are below.
See how each family is alike
To see where each animal should go.

Point to where each animal should go
Then tell me why you know it's so.

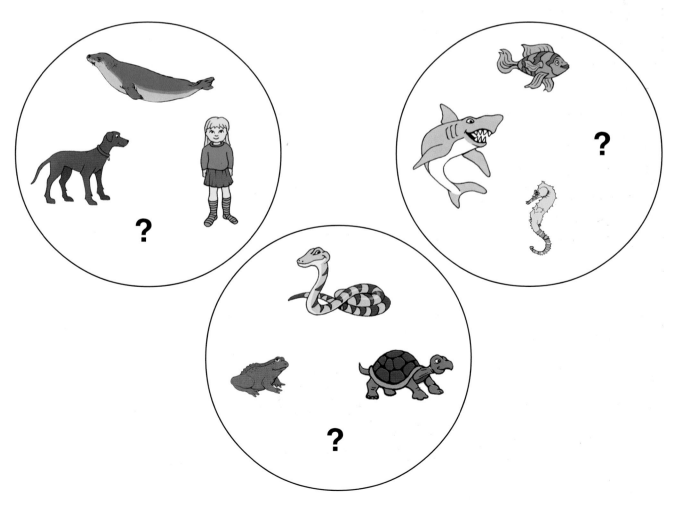

Even though the ribbon was still tied
Ed figured out a clock was inside.
Which of his senses did Ed use?
Point to the one that you would choose.

Mother called, "Come on, sleepyhead
It's time to hop out of that warm bed."
Allen could tell without even looking
That it was bacon that Mom was cooking.

Which of his senses did Allen use?
Tell me which one you would choose.

These are not fish

But they live in the sea.

They can't breathe underwater

Which three must they be?

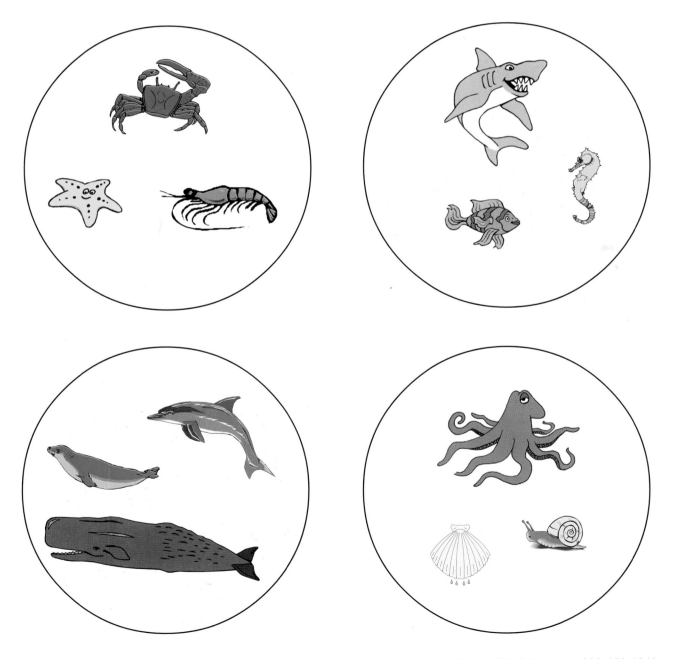

When I turn on the wall switch

The light shines bright.

When I turn off the wall switch

The room is dark as night.

Look at each picture so you can see

If the switch's on or off then tell me.

Is the wall switch on or off?

Is the wall switch on or off?

Is the wall switch on or off?

Is the wall switch on or off?

I warn you it's poison
Don't touch me, stay away!
Tell your parents when you see me
And they'll make it safe to play.

Of the three pictures that you see
Tell me now, can you find me?

I like to eat burgers
I like to eat fries.
When I eat too much
I grow in size.

Put these pictures in order
One, two, three and four.
I started out hungry
Now I can't eat anymore.

Max Magoo   Leslie Lu

Two pictures below are Max Magoo

Two pictures below are Leslie Lu.

Look at their pictures

And tell me who's who.

I am a place to go
When you want to eat.
You look at the menu
When you take a seat.

Of the four things that you see
Tell me now, can you find me?

I am on the right
And I have lost a shoe.
I have both my socks
I'm dressed in orange and blue.

Of the four people that you see
Tell me now, can you find me?

I am dressed for winter
For a walk through the snow.
It's nighttime in the woods
But the sky is all aglow.

Of the four pictures that you see
Tell me now, can you find me?

I am a mommy

My daughter has brown hair.

She has two daughters

Sue Ann and little Claire.

Look at the people in my family

Then tell me now, can you find me?

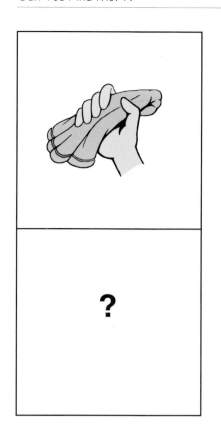

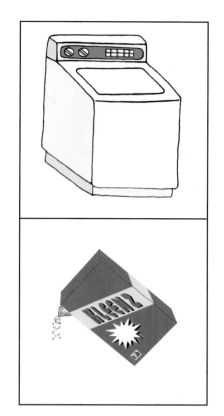

?

Look at each pair of pictures
There's always two of a kind.
See how each pair is alike
Then you'll know what to find.

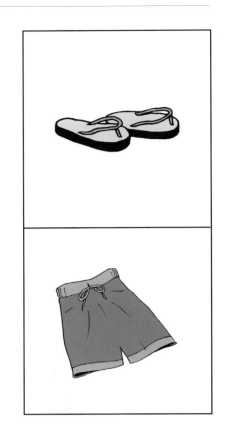

Look at each pair of pictures
There's always two of a kind.

See how each pair is alike
Then you'll know what to find.

The bag tipped over
And spilled on the floor.
What must have happened
To the bag just before?

The moon was rising
It was round and bright.
Then two clouds appeared
In the star-filled night.

Which pair of pictures that you see
Tells what happened in this story?

Stay away from me

When you see who I am.

I warn you of danger

Whenever I can.

Of the three pictures that you see

Tell me now, can you find me?

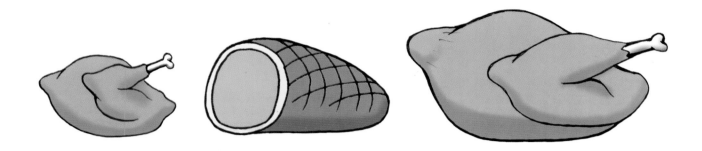

I can hold a chicken
I can hold a ham.
I can hold a turkey
I'm called a roasting pan.

Of the four pans that you see
Tell me now, can you find me?

Tim took a few minutes

Jill and Tom took an hour.

Sue took all morning long

To climb the water tower.

They all left together

Never stopping to quench their thirst.

Which of these four climbers

Reached the top of the tower first?

Sue   Tim   Jill   Tom

When she hears the ring

She runs to the door.

But can you tell me

What happened just before?

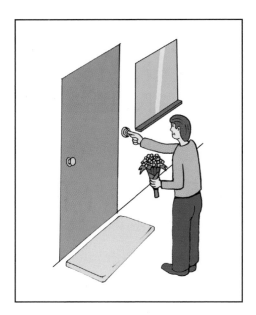

She is not my older sister

We were born on the same day.

We have two younger sisters

Mary Sue and Carrie May.

Of all the sisters in my family

Which two must the two of us be?

I am not the first
But I am close to C.
I am next to F
But I am not G.

Of the letters that you see
Tell me now, can you find me?

A B C D E F G

Of the four letters
That you see
Put them in order
Alphabetically.

 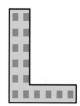  

Say  and

The first sound is the same.

Say  and

What's this first letter's name?

Say  and

The first sound is the same.

Say  and

What's this first letter's name?

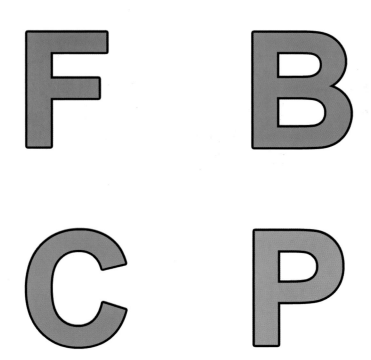

Say  and

The first sound is the same.

Say  and

What is this letter's name?

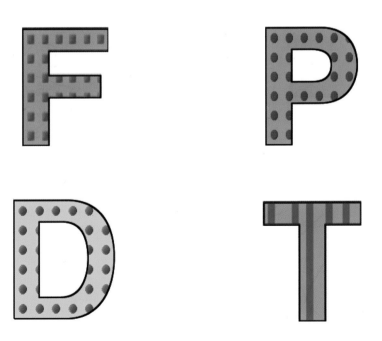

All these words begin the same
All except for one.
Find the word that doesn't fit
Then you will be done.

nut   **map**   **nap**   **nose**

All these words begin the same
All except for one.
Find the word that doesn't fit
Then you will be done.

ball   bag   dig   bee

All these words begin the same
All except for one.
Find the word that doesn't fit
Then you will be done.

sink   sand   fan   soap

Rhyming words sound alike
Except how they begin.
Like box and fox, hand and sand
And also fin and win.

Find a word that rhymes with cot
and also rhymes with not and hot.

hat

hop

pot

Rhyming words sound the same
Words like lame, tame, and name.
Find the word that rhymes with chime
And also climb, time, and dime.

game

light

lime

Rhyming words have the same sound
Words like found, mound, pound and round.
Look for a word like hope and slope
The word below that rhymes with rope.

sew

soap

road

© 2003 Critical Thinking Books & Software • www.CriticalThinking.com • 800-458-4849

Listen for the sound
Listen carefully.
I begin each word
Which letter must I be?

Listen for the sound
Listen carefully.
I begin each word
Which letter must I be?

CKS

Listen for the sound
Listen carefully.
I begin each word
What letter must I be?

long   little   light   ?

man   motor   might   ?

kick   kindly   kite   ?

win   wicked   white   ?

In this group is a brown moose

On top of him sits a white goose.

Underneath the moose is a gray rat

And beside the rat is a brown bat.

Of the four groups that you see

Which group must these four be?

Listen for the last sound
Listen carefully.
I'm at the end of each word
Which letter must I be?

Listen for the last sound
Listen carefully.
I'm at the end of each word
Which letter must I be?

Listen for the last sound

Listen carefully.

I'm at the end of each word

Which letter must I be?

There once was an ogre
Who had a naughty dog.
It chased a little piglet
Till it met an angry hog.

Of the four pictures that you see
Which shows the end of this story?

I am found in the middle
Of run, cup, and bug.
I am found in the middle
Of sun, pup, and hug.

Of the four letters that you see
Tell me now, can you find me?

I am found in the middle
Of map, cat, and ran.
I am found in the middle
Of mad, ham, and fan.

Of the four letters that you see
Tell me now, can you find me?

i   a

u   e

I am found in the middle
Of big, pin, and sit.
I am found in the middle
Of lid, sip, and hit.

Of the four letters that you see
Tell me now, can you find me?

It is the color
Of cloudless skies
A pond and a lake
And my best friend's eyes.

Of the four words that you see
Tell me now, can you find me?

yellow   **red**

green   **blue**

I am found in pin
But not in bat.
I am found in win
But not in cat.

Of the four letters that you see
Tell me now, can you find me?

Rhyming words sound the same

Words like name, tame, and game.

Find the word that rhymes below

With the two words go and throw.

hoe   catch   home

Rhyming words sound the same
Words like name, tame, and game.
Listen to sing, ring and wing
Which word below rhymes with thing?

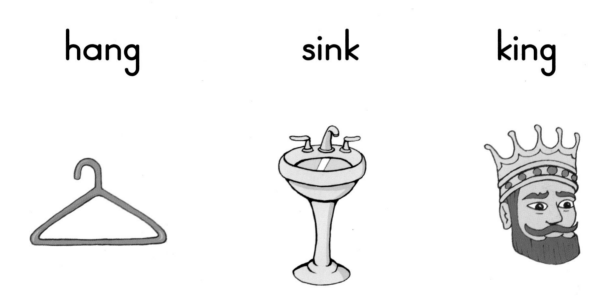

hang   sink   king

I am found in cat
I am found in rat.
You can hear my name
When you say cake and game.

Of the four letters that you see
Tell me now, can you find me?

e   o

a   i

ANSWERS

MATH (pp.1–34)

1. boy on the right
2. red-haired girl on left
3. The square on the lower right is rotated.
4. 1
5. 4 pigs (lower right)
6. Jan, her friend, is in the green dress.
7. boy on lower right
8. square and rectangle
9. medium yellow circle (increasing size pattern)
10. group of 2 blocks on lower left
11. 4
12. 7 (introduces greater than)
13. dogs (lower left)
14. boy on lower right
15. beach ball (pattern: small, large, large)
16. apples (lower left)
17. middle girl in middle row on right
18. shape pattern (square, triangle, square)
19. group of 7 blue blocks on lower right
20. Jeremy (count the amount of money, not the number of coins)
21. quarter apple
22. 2 shirts (navy and red shirts in the overlapping section)
23. 2 socks (purple and green in the overlapping section)
24. Bill ate half a cookie
25. color pattern (yellow, red)
26. blackboard (rectangle)
27. green car is third from the gate
28. green pentagon on left, pink square on right, yellow rectangle in middle
29. group in lower left box
30. 1 blue dot (machine eats green dots)
31. 6 dots on left (machine doubles the number of dots)
32. 8 oranges (The middle glass is twice as tall as the short glass.)
33. boy on lower left
34. group on lower right

SCIENCE (pp. 35–57)

35. sun and rain (or water)
36. 1) caterpillar, 2) cocoon, 3) butterfly
37. melted popsicle in middle (effect of heat)
38. puppy (mother/child relationship)
39. turtle (number of legs)
40. 1) summer (or spring), 2) fall, 3) winter
41. teeth
42. camel/desert, cow/farm, deer/forest
43. shark on upper right
44. 1) building nest, 2) sitting on eggs, 3) hatching birds
45. ostrich
46. hawk by the road (food chain)
47. seal (A seal and fish both move in water.)
48. ice cube (Both ice cube and rock are solids.)
49. cheetah (pattern is increasing speed)
50. whale (pattern is increasing size)
51. centipede (pattern is increasing number of legs)
52. bottom row
53. cow, upper left (mammals); lizard, lower middle (reptiles); fish, upper right
54. ear (Ed heard the clock ticking.)
55. nose (Allen smelled bacon cooking.)
56. mammals (lower left)

57. The wall switch is on in the lower left and lower right pictures.

SOCIAL STUDIES (pp. 58–73)

58. poison symbol in center

59. 1) he is hungry (lower left); 2) he is ready to eat (upper left); 3) he is eating (lower right); 4) he is full (upper right)

60. Max (figures 1 and 4), Leslie (figures 2 and 3)

61. restaurant (lower left)

62. boy on lower right

63. boy on lower left

64. grandmother

65. soap (things used together to clean)

66. mittens (clothes worn together in different weather)

67. The cat spilled the bag. (lower left picture)

68. last row

69. symbol on left

70. roasting pan on lower right

71. Tim

72. He rings the doorbell. (picture on upper right)

73. Figures 2 and 5 (from left to right) are the older twins.

READING (pp. 74–100)

74. E

75. L M N O

76. F (fire, fish, fox, feather)

77. P (pig, pumpkin, pins, pizza)

78. T (tie, turtle, tent, toaster)

79. map

80. dig

81. fan

82. pot

83. lime

84. soap

85. F, G

86. D, S

87. l, m, k, w

88. group at upper right

89. T, M

90. G, P

91. D, N

92. hog on dog, lower right

93. u

94. a

95. i

96. blue

97. i

98. hoe

99. king

100. a

MATH SKILLS MATRIX

	1	2	3	4	5	6	7	8	9	10	11	12	13	14	15	16	17	18	19	20	21	22	23	24	25	26	27	28	29	30	31	32	33	34
MATH																																		
Addition/subtraction				■	■					■									■		■			■						■	■	■		
Counting	■			■	■	■	■	■		■	■	■	■			■	■		■	■		■	■				■			■	■	■	■	
Fractions, part-whole																				■				■										■
Graphs, charts													■				■				■	■												
Measurement		■											■																			■		
Money																				■														
More/less, greater		■			■					■	■	■	■			■			■	■											■			
Number recognition				■							■	■																						
Number sequence											■	■																						
Ordinal numbers						■																					■							
Patterns									■						■			■							■									
Shape recognition			■				■	■							■			■							■	■		■						
Spatial position	■		■				■	■						■			■										■		■					
THINKING SKILLS																																		
CLASSIFICATION																																		
Find common attribute									■													■	■		■		■		■	■				
Find the exception			■																															
Identify category									■																	■		■						
Sort objects																■				■		■	■					■						
SIMILARITIES/DIFF																																		
Compare objects	■	■	■		■		■				■	■	■	■	■	■	■	■	■	■	■	■	■	■		■		■	■			■	■	■
Find two the same			■					■																										
SEQUENCE																																		
Complete a pattern									■						■																			
Identify a pattern									■						■			■												■	■			
Rank by size, degree		■				■			■	■			■			■									■		■							
Series of steps, events																				■			■										■	
ANALOGY																																		
Opposites/Similarities																										■								
LOGIC																																		
And/or, but not, if/then										■												■	■							■	■			■

Based on the National Math Standards

SCIENCE SKILLS MATRIX

	35	36	37	38	39	40	41	42	43	44	45	46	47	48	49	50	51	52	53	54	55	56	57
SCIENCE																							
Animals		■		■	■		■	■	■	■	■	■	■		■	■	■		■			■	
Body parts					■		■		■						■	■				■	■		
Cause/effect			■																				■
Plants	■																						
Properties of objects			■	■	■						■		■	■	■								
Seasons/weather						■												■					
Senses																				■	■		
THINKING SKILLS																							
CLASSIFICATION																							
Find common attribute				■	■								■	■	■				■			■	
Find the exception																							
Identify category					■														■				
Sort objects					■	■							■	■					■				
SIMILARITIES/DIFF																							
Compare objects	■			■	■		■	■	■		■		■	■	■	■	■			■	■	■	■
Find two the same					■								■										
SEQUENCE																							
Complete a pattern				■		■									■	■	■						
Identify a pattern		■		■						■					■	■	■	■					
Put in order		■				■				■		■											
Rank by size, degree															■	■	■						
Series of steps, events		■	■			■				■		■						■					
ANALOGY																							
Opposites/Similarities				■	■								■	■									
LOGIC																							
And/or, but not, if/then																							■

SOCIAL STUDIES SKILLS MATRIX

	58	59	60	61	62	63	64	65	66	67	68	69	70	71	72	73
SOCIAL STUDIES																
Cause/effect		■								■					■	
Clothing, food, shelter		■	■	■	■	■			■				■			
Community/home	■		■				■					■			■	
Family							■									■
Health/Safety	■											■				
Location words					■											
Seasons/weather						■			■		■					
Time						■				■	■			■	■	
Tools, symbols	■							■				■	■			
THINKING SKILLS																
CLASSIFICATION																
Find common attribute								■	■							■
Identify category				■				■	■							
Sort objects								■	■							
SIMILARITIES/DIFF																
Compare objects	■		■	■	■		■	■	■		■	■	■	■		■
Find two the same			■													■
SEQUENCE																
Put in order		■					■			■						
Rank by size, degree														■		
Series of steps, events		■								■	■			■	■	
ANALOGY																
Used to, association								■	■							
LOGIC																
And/or, but not, if/then						■										

READING SKILLS MATRIX

	74	75	76	77	78	79	80	81	82	83	84	85	86	87	88	89	90	91	92	93	94	95	96	97	98	99	100
READING																											
Alphabet sequence	■	■																									
Auditory discrimination			■	■	■	■	■	■	■	■	■	■	■	■		■	■	■		■	■	■		■	■	■	■
Fantasy/reality															■				■								
Letter recognition	■	■	■	■	■							■	■	■		■	■	■		■	■	■		■			■
Letter/sound assn.			■	■	■	■	■	■				■	■	■		■	■	■		■	■	■		■			■
Rhyming words									■	■	■														■	■	
Sight words																							■				
Spatial orientation	■	■										■	■		■	■	■	■									
Visual discrimination	■	■	■	■	■							■	■	■	■	■	■	■		■	■	■	■	■			■
THINKING SKILLS																											
CLASSIFICATION																											
Find common attribute			■	■	■	■	■	■	■	■	■	■	■	■		■	■	■							■	■	
Find the exception						■	■	■																			
Identify category			■	■	■	■	■	■				■	■	■		■	■	■									
Sort objects						■	■	■																			
SIMILARITIES/DIFF																											
Compare objects			■	■	■	■	■	■	■	■	■	■	■	■	■	■	■	■		■	■	■		■	■	■	■
SEQUENCE																											
Identify a pattern		■																									
Put in order		■													■				■								
Series of steps, events															■				■								